MY LITTLE QUOTEBOOK

Because every
quote tells a
story...

When was it said? _____

Where? _____

How would you describe it?

Funny ☐   Profound ☐   Silly ☐   Bizarre ☐

Age? _____

When was it said? _____ Age? ___

Where? _____

"

Funny ☐ Profound ☐ Silly ☐ Bizarre ☐

When was it said? _____ Age? ___

Where? _____

"

Funny ☐ Profound ☐ Silly ☐ Bizarre ☐

When was it said? _____

Where? _____

How would you describe it?

Funny ☐   Profound ☐   Silly ☐   Bizarre ☐

Age? ☐

When was it said? _____ Age?

Where? _____

"

Funny ☐   Profound ☐   silly ☐   Bizarre ☐

When was it said? _____ Age?

Where? _____

"

Funny ☐   Profound ☐   silly ☐   Bizarre ☐

When was it said? _____

Where? _____

How would you describe it?

Funny ☐   Profound ☐   Silly ☐   Bizarre ☐

Age? _____

When was it said? _____ Age? _____

Where? _____

"

Funny ☐   Profound ☐   Silly ☐   Bizarre ☐

When was it said? _____ Age? _____

Where? _____

"

Funny ☐   Profound ☐   Silly ☐   Bizarre ☐

When was it said? _____

Where? _____

How would you describe it?

Funny ☐   Profound ☐   Silly ☐   Bizarre ☐

Age? ☐

When was it said? _____ ⌐ Age? ⌐
        Where? _____

"
        _____

        Funny ☐   Profound ☐   Silly ☐   Bizarre ☐
"

When was it said? _____ ⌐ Age? ⌐
        Where? _____

"
        _____

        Funny ☐   Profound ☐   Silly ☐   Bizarre ☐
"

When was it said? _____

Where? _____

"

How would you describe it?

Funny ☐   Profound ☐   Silly ☐   Bizarre ☐

☆   Age? _____   ☆

When was it said? _____ Age? _____

Where? _____

"

Funny ☐ Profound ☐ Silly ☐ Bizarre ☐

When was it said? _____ Age? _____

Where? _____

"

Funny ☐ Profound ☐ Silly ☐ Bizarre ☐

When was it said? _____

Where? _____

"

"

How would you describe it?

Funny ☐   Profound ☐   Silly ☐   Bizarre ☐

Age? ☐

When was it said? _____ Age?

Where? _____

"

"

Funny ☐   Profound ☐   silly ☐   Bizarre ☐

When was it said? _____ Age?

Where? _____

"

"

Funny ☐   Profound ☐   silly ☐   Bizarre ☐

When was it said? _____

Where? _____

"

"

How would you describe it?

Funny ☐   Profound ☐   Silly ☐   Bizarre ☐

Age? _____

When was it said? _____ ⌐ Age? ⌐

Where? _____

"

Funny ☐   Profound ☐   Silly ☐   Bizarre ☐

When was it said? _____ ⌐ Age? ⌐

Where? _____

"

Funny ☐   Profound ☐   Silly ☐   Bizarre ☐

When was it said? _____

Where? _____

How would you describe it?

Funny ☐   Profound ☐   Silly ☐   Bizarre ☐

Age? _____

When was it said? _____ Age?

Where? _____

"

Funny ☐   Profound ☐   Silly ☐   Bizarre ☐

When was it said? _____ Age?

Where? _____

"

Funny ☐   Profound ☐   Silly ☐   Bizarre ☐

When was it said? _____

Where? _____

How would you describe it?

Funny ☐   Profound ☐   Silly ☐   Bizarre ☐

Age? ☐

When was it said? _____ Age? _____

Where? _____

"

Funny ☐   Profound ☐   Silly ☐   Bizarre ☐

"

When was it said? _____ Age? _____

Where? _____

"

Funny ☐   Profound ☐   Silly ☐   Bizarre ☐

"

When was it said? _____

Where? _____

"

"

How would you describe it?

Funny ☐   Profound ☐   Silly ☐   Bizarre ☐

Age? _____

When was it said? _____ Age?

Where? _____

"

Funny ☐   Profound ☐   Silly ☐   Bizarre ☐

"

When was it said? _____ Age?

Where? _____

"

Funny ☐   Profound ☐   Silly ☐   Bizarre ☐

"

When was it said? _____

Where? _____

How would you describe it?

Funny ☐   Profound ☐   Silly ☐   Bizarre ☐

Age? _____

When was it said? _____ Age?

Where? _____

"

Funny ☐   Profound ☐   Silly ☐   Bizarre ☐

When was it said? _____ Age?

Where? _____

"

Funny ☐   Profound ☐   Silly ☐   Bizarre ☐

When was it said? _____

Where? _____

"

"

How would you describe it?

Funny ☐   Profound ☐   Silly ☐   Bizarre ☐

Age? _____

When was it said? _____ ⌐ Age? ¬

Where? _____

"

Funny ☐   Profound ☐   Silly ☐   Bizarre ☐

♡   ☆   ♡   ☆   ♡

When was it said? _____ ⌐ Age? ¬

Where? _____

"

Funny ☐   Profound ☐   Silly ☐   Bizarre ☐

When was it said? _____

Where? _____

"

"

How would you describe it?

Funny ☐   Profound ☐   Silly ☐   Bizarre ☐

Age? _____

When was it said? _____ Age? _____

Where? _____

" _____

Funny ☐ Profound ☐ Silly ☐ Bizarre ☐

When was it said? _____ Age? _____

Where? _____

" _____

Funny ☐ Profound ☐ Silly ☐ Bizarre ☐

When was it said? _____

Where? _____

How would you describe it?

Funny ☐   Profound ☐   Silly ☐   Bizarre ☐

Age? ☐

When was it said? _____ Age?

Where? _____

"

Funny ☐   Profound ☐   Silly ☐   Bizarre ☐

When was it said? _____ Age?

Where? _____

"

Funny ☐   Profound ☐   Silly ☐   Bizarre ☐

When was it said? _____

Where? _____

How would you describe it?

Funny ☐ Profound ☐ Silly ☐ Bizarre ☐

Age? _____

When was it said? _____ Age? _____

Where? _____

"

Funny ☐ Profound ☐ Silly ☐ Bizarre ☐

"

When was it said? _____ Age? _____

Where? _____

"

Funny ☐ Profound ☐ Silly ☐ Bizarre ☐

"

When was it said? _____

Where? _____

"

"

How would you describe it?

Funny ☐   Profound ☐   Silly ☐   Bizarre ☐

Age? [ ]

☆   ☆

When was it said? _____ Age? _____

"Where? _____

Funny ☐   Profound ☐   silly ☐   Bizarre ☐

When was it said? _____ Age? _____

"Where? _____

Funny ☐   Profound ☐   silly ☐   Bizarre ☐

When was it said? _____

Where? _____

"

"

How would you describe it?

Funny ☐   Profound ☐   silly ☐   Bizarre ☐

Age?

When was it said? _____ Age? ___

Where? _____

"

Funny ☐   Profound ☐   Silly ☐   Bizarre ☐

When was it said? _____ Age? ___

Where? _____

"

Funny ☐   Profound ☐   Silly ☐   Bizarre ☐

When was it said? _____

Where? _____

"

"

How would you describe it?

Funny ☐   Profound ☐   Silly ☐   Bizarre ☐

Age? _____

When was it said? _____ ⌐ Age? ⌐

Where? _____

" "

Funny ☐   Profound ☐   Silly ☐   Bizarre ☐

When was it said? _____ ⌐ Age? ⌐

Where? _____

" "

Funny ☐   Profound ☐   Silly ☐   Bizarre ☐

When was it said? _____

Where? _____

How would you describe it?

Funny ☐   Profound ☐   Silly ☐   Bizarre ☐

Age? _____

When was it said? _____ Age? _____

Where? _____

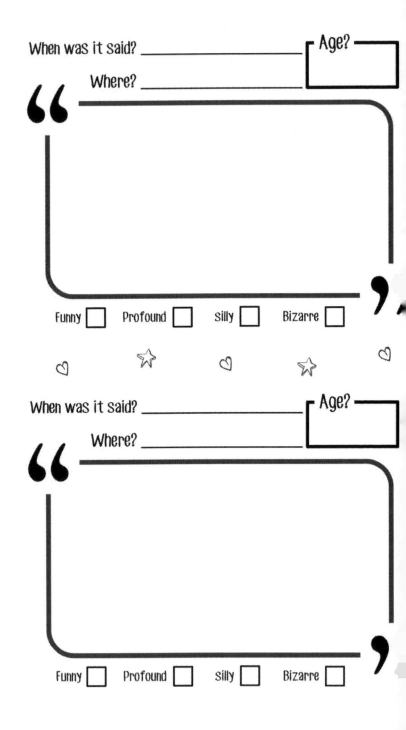

Funny ☐   Profound ☐   Silly ☐   Bizarre ☐

When was it said? _____ Age? _____

Where? _____

Funny ☐   Profound ☐   Silly ☐   Bizarre ☐

When was it said? _____

Where? _____

How would you describe it?

Funny ☐   Profound ☐   Silly ☐   Bizarre ☐

Age? _____

When was it said? _____ Age? _____

Where? _____

"

Funny ☐   Profound ☐   Silly ☐   Bizarre ☐

When was it said? _____ Age? _____

Where? _____

"

Funny ☐   Profound ☐   Silly ☐   Bizarre ☐

When was it said? _____

Where? _____

How would you describe it?

Funny ☐   Profound ☐   Silly ☐   Bizarre ☐

Age? [_____]

When was it said? _____ Age? _____

Where? _____

"

Funny ☐   Profound ☐   Silly ☐   Bizarre ☐

"

When was it said? _____ Age? _____

Where? _____

"

Funny ☐   Profound ☐   Silly ☐   Bizarre ☐

"

When was it said? _____

Where? _____

How would you describe it?

Funny ☐   Profound ☐   Silly ☐   Bizarre ☐

Age? _____

When was it said? _____ Age? _____

Where? _____

"

Funny ☐ Profound ☐ silly ☐ Bizarre ☐

When was it said? _____ Age? _____

Where? _____

"

Funny ☐ Profound ☐ silly ☐ Bizarre ☐

When was it said? _____

Where? _____

" "

How would you describe it?

Funny ☐   Profound ☐   Silly ☐   Bizarre ☐

Age? ☐

When was it said? _____ Age? ___

Where? _____

"

Funny ☐   Profound ☐   Silly ☐   Bizarre ☐

When was it said? _____ Age? ___

Where? _____

"

Funny ☐   Profound ☐   Silly ☐   Bizarre ☐

When was it said? _____

Where? _____

"

"

How would you describe it?

Funny ☐   Profound ☐   Silly ☐   Bizarre ☐

Age?

When was it said? _____ Age?

Where? _____

"

Funny ☐   Profound ☐   Silly ☐   Bizarre ☐

"

When was it said? _____ Age?

Where? _____

"

Funny ☐   Profound ☐   Silly ☐   Bizarre ☐

"

When was it said? _____

Where? _____

How would you describe it?

Funny ☐   Profound ☐   Silly ☐   Bizarre ☐

Age? _____

When was it said? _____ ⌐ Age? ¬

Where? _____

"

Funny ☐ Profound ☐ Silly ☐ Bizarre ☐

When was it said? _____ ⌐ Age? ¬

Where? _____

"

Funny ☐ Profound ☐ Silly ☐ Bizarre ☐

When was it said? _____

Where? _____

How would you describe it?

Funny ☐   Profound ☐   Silly ☐   Bizarre ☐

Age? _____

When was it said? _____ Age? _____

Where? _____

"

Funny ☐ Profound ☐ Silly ☐ Bizarre ☐

When was it said? _____ Age? _____

Where? _____

"

Funny ☐ Profound ☐ Silly ☐ Bizarre ☐

When was it said? _____

Where? _____

99

66

How would you describe it?

Funny ☐   Profound ☐   Silly ☐   Bizarre ☐

☆   Age? ☐   ☆

When was it said? _____ ┌─ Age? ─┐

Where? _____

"

Funny ☐   Profound ☐   Silly ☐   Bizarre ☐

When was it said? _____ ┌─ Age? ─┐

Where? _____

"

Funny ☐   Profound ☐   Silly ☐   Bizarre ☐

When was it said? _____

Where? _____

"

"

How would you describe it?

Funny ☐   Profound ☐   Silly ☐   Bizarre ☐

Age? _____

When was it said? _____ Age?

Where? _____

"

Funny ☐ Profound ☐ Silly ☐ Bizarre ☐

"

When was it said? _____ Age?

Where? _____

"

Funny ☐ Profound ☐ Silly ☐ Bizarre ☐

"

When was it said? _____

Where? _____

"

How would you describe it?

Funny ☐   Profound ☐   Silly ☐   Bizarre ☐

Age? _____

When was it said? _____ ⌐ Age? ⌐

Where? _____

"

Funny ☐   Profound ☐   silly ☐   Bizarre ☐

When was it said? _____ ⌐ Age? ⌐

Where? _____

"

Funny ☐   Profound ☐   silly ☐   Bizarre ☐

When was it said? _____

Where? _____

"

"

How would you describe it?

Funny ☐   Profound ☐   Silly ☐   Bizarre ☐

Age? _____

When was it said? _____ Age? [   ]

Where? _____

"

Funny [ ]   Profound [ ]   Silly [ ]   Bizarre [ ]

"

When was it said? _____ Age? [   ]

Where? _____

"

Funny [ ]   Profound [ ]   Silly [ ]   Bizarre [ ]

"

When was it said? _____

Where? _____

"

How would you describe it?

Funny ☐   Profound ☐   silly ☐   Bizarre ☐

Age? ☐

When was it said? _____ ⌐ Age? ⌐

Where? _____

" "

Funny ☐   Profound ☐   Silly ☐   Bizarre ☐

When was it said? _____ ⌐ Age? ⌐

Where? _____

" "

Funny ☐   Profound ☐   Silly ☐   Bizarre ☐

When was it said? _____

Where? _____

"

How would you describe it?

Funny ☐   Profound ☐   Silly ☐   Bizarre ☐

Age? ☐

When was it said? _____ ⌐ Age? ⌐

Where? _____

" "

Funny ☐   Profound ☐   Silly ☐   Bizarre ☐

When was it said? _____ ⌐ Age? ⌐

Where? _____

" "

Funny ☐   Profound ☐   Silly ☐   Bizarre ☐

When was it said? _____

Where? _____

How would you describe it?

Funny ☐   Profound ☐   Silly ☐   Bizarre ☐

Age? _____

When was it said? _____ Age?

Where? _____

"

Funny ☐   Profound ☐   Silly ☐   Bizarre ☐

When was it said? _____ Age?

Where? _____

"

Funny ☐   Profound ☐   Silly ☐   Bizarre ☐

When was it said? _____

Where? _____

"

How would you describe it?

Funny ☐   Profound ☐   Silly ☐   Bizarre ☐

Age? _____

When was it said? _____ Age? ____

Where? _____

" "

Funny ☐   Profound ☐   Silly ☐   Bizarre ☐

When was it said? _____ Age? ____

Where? _____

" "

Funny ☐   Profound ☐   Silly ☐   Bizarre ☐

When was it said? _____

Where? _____

99

66

How would you describe it?

Funny ☐   Profound ☐   Silly ☐   Bizarre ☐

Age? ☐

When was it said? _____ Age? [   ]

Where? _____

"

Funny [   ]   Profound [   ]   Silly [   ]   Bizarre [   ]

When was it said? _____ Age? [   ]

Where? _____

"

Funny [   ]   Profound [   ]   Silly [   ]   Bizarre [   ]

When was it said? _____

Where? _____

"

How would you describe it?

Funny ☐   Profound ☐   Silly ☐   Bizarre ☐

Age? _____

When was it said? _____ Age? _____

Where? _____

"

Funny ☐   Profound ☐   Silly ☐   Bizarre ☐

"

When was it said? _____ Age? _____

Where? _____

"

Funny ☐   Profound ☐   Silly ☐   Bizarre ☐

"

When was it said? _____

Where? _____

How would you describe it?

Funny ☐   Profound ☐   Silly ☐   Bizarre ☐

Age? _____

When was it said? _____ Age?

Where? _____

"

Funny ☐   Profound ☐   Silly ☐   Bizarre ☐

When was it said? _____ Age?

Where? _____

"

Funny ☐   Profound ☐   Silly ☐   Bizarre ☐

When was it said? _____

Where? _____

"

"

How would you describe it?

Funny ☐   Profound ☐   silly ☐   Bizarre ☐

☆   Age? _____   ☆

When was it said? _____ Age? _____

Where? _____

"

Funny ☐　　Profound ☐　　Silly ☐　　Bizarre ☐

"

When was it said? _____ Age? _____

Where? _____

"

Funny ☐　　Profound ☐　　Silly ☐　　Bizarre ☐

"

When was it said? _____

Where? _____

"

How would you describe it?

Funny ☐   Profound ☐   Silly ☐   Bizarre ☐

Age? _____

When was it said? _____ Age?

Where? _____

"

Funny ☐ Profound ☐ Silly ☐ Bizarre ☐

When was it said? _____ Age?

Where? _____

"

Funny ☐ Profound ☐ Silly ☐ Bizarre ☐

When was it said? _____

Where? _____

,,

"

How would you describe it?

Funny ☐   Profound ☐   Silly ☐   Bizarre ☐

Age? [_____]

When was it said? _____ ⌐ Age? ⌐
  Where? _____

"

Funny ☐ Profound ☐ Silly ☐ Bizarre ☐ "

When was it said? _____ ⌐ Age? ⌐
  Where? _____

"

Funny ☐ Profound ☐ Silly ☐ Bizarre ☐ "

When was it said? _____

Where? _____

How would you describe it?

Funny ☐   Profound ☐   Silly ☐   Bizarre ☐

Age? _____

When was it said? _____

Where? _____

Age?

"

"

Funny ☐ Profound ☐ Silly ☐ Bizarre ☐

When was it said? _____

Where? _____

Age?

"

"

Funny ☐ Profound ☐ Silly ☐ Bizarre ☐

When was it said? _____

Where? _____

"

"

How would you describe it?

Funny ☐   Profound ☐   Silly ☐   Bizarre ☐

Age? ☐

When was it said? _____ Age?

Where? _____

"

Funny ☐   Profound ☐   Silly ☐   Bizarre ☐

When was it said? _____ Age?

Where? _____

"

Funny ☐   Profound ☐   Silly ☐   Bizarre ☐

When was it said? _____

Where? _____

"

"

How would you describe it?

Funny ☐　　Profound ☐　　Silly ☐　　Bizarre ☐

☆　　Age? _____　　☆

When was it said? _____ Age? _____

Where? _____

"

Funny ☐   Profound ☐   Silly ☐   Bizarre ☐

When was it said? _____ Age? _____

Where? _____

"

Funny ☐   Profound ☐   Silly ☐   Bizarre ☐

When was it said? _____

Where? _____

How would you describe it?

Funny ☐   Profound ☐   Silly ☐   Bizarre ☐

Age? _____

When was it said? _____ Age? _____

Where? _____

"

Funny ☐ Profound ☐ Silly ☐ Bizarre ☐

"

When was it said? _____ Age? _____

Where? _____

"

Funny ☐ Profound ☐ Silly ☐ Bizarre ☐

"

When was it said? _____

Where? _____

How would you describe it?

Funny ☐   Profound ☐   Silly ☐   Bizarre ☐

Age? _____

When was it said? _____

Age? _____

Where? _____

"

"

Funny ☐ Profound ☐ Silly ☐ Bizarre ☐

When was it said? _____

Age? _____

Where? _____

"

"

Funny ☐ Profound ☐ Silly ☐ Bizarre ☐

When was it said? _____

Where? _____

"

"

How would you describe it?

Funny ☐   Profound ☐   Silly ☐   Bizarre ☐

Age? _____

When was it said? _____ Age? _____

Where? _____

" "

Funny ☐ Profound ☐ Silly ☐ Bizarre ☐

When was it said? _____ Age? _____

Where? _____

" "

Funny ☐ Profound ☐ Silly ☐ Bizarre ☐

When was it said? _____

Where? _____

How would you describe it?

Funny ☐   Profound ☐   Silly ☐   Bizarre ☐

Age? _____

When was it said? _____ Age?

Where? _____

"

Funny ☐   Profound ☐   Silly ☐   Bizarre ☐

When was it said? _____ Age?

Where? _____

"

Funny ☐   Profound ☐   Silly ☐   Bizarre ☐

When was it said? _____

Where? _____

"

How would you describe it?

Funny ☐   Profound ☐   Silly ☐   Bizarre ☐

Age? ☐

When was it said? _____ ┌─ Age? ─┐

Where? _____

"

Funny ☐   Profound ☐   Silly ☐   Bizarre ☐

When was it said? _____ ┌─ Age? ─┐

Where? _____

"

Funny ☐   Profound ☐   Silly ☐   Bizarre ☐

When was it said? _____

Where? _____

How would you describe it?

Funny ☐   Profound ☐   Silly ☐   Bizarre ☐

Age? _____

When was it said? _____ Age?

Where? _____

"

Funny ☐ Profound ☐ Silly ☐ Bizarre ☐

"

When was it said? _____ Age?

Where? _____

"

Funny ☐ Profound ☐ Silly ☐ Bizarre ☐

"

When was it said? _____

Where? _____

How would you describe it?

Funny ☐   Profound ☐   Silly ☐   Bizarre ☐

Age? _____

When was it said? _____ Age? _____

Where? _____

" "

Funny ☐ Profound ☐ Silly ☐ Bizarre ☐

When was it said? _____ Age? _____

Where? _____

" "

Funny ☐ Profound ☐ Silly ☐ Bizarre ☐

When was it said? _____

Where? _____

How would you describe it?

Funny ☐   Profound ☐   Silly ☐   Bizarre ☐

Age? _____

When was it said? _____ Age? _____

Where? _____

"

Funny ☐   Profound ☐   Silly ☐   Bizarre ☐

♡   ☆   ♡   ☆   ♡

When was it said? _____ Age? _____

Where? _____

"

Funny ☐   Profound ☐   Silly ☐   Bizarre ☐

When was it said? _____

Where? _____

How would you describe it?

Funny ☐   Profound ☐   Silly ☐   Bizarre ☐

Age? ☐

When was it said? _____ Age?

Where? _____

"

Funny ☐   Profound ☐   Silly ☐   Bizarre ☐

"

When was it said? _____ Age?

Where? _____

"

Funny ☐   Profound ☐   Silly ☐   Bizarre ☐

"